To my parents, and to the Bush Foundation and Cheryl Prentice who supported my work on proverbs. — A.H.

To my parents who have always supported me. — W.E.

To my husband, John, for believing, encouraging, and understanding me through this incredible artistic journey. — M.T.

Special thanks to Sherry Bushue and Jenn Bailey from The Little Fig who saw the potential in this book and worked tirelessly to see it published. Thanks to Carol Hinz who provided feedback on an early manuscript and to the members of the Shoreview Scribblers Critique Group for their critiques and support. — A.H. & W.E.

the little fig®

www.thelittlefig.com

Fire and Ashes:
A Boy and an African Proverb

Ninna dab buu ka baqaa, ninna dambaas buu ka baqaa.
One man fears fire; another man fears ashes.

By Ahmed Hassan and Wes Erwin
Illustrator Meryl Treatner

Warfa ran his fingers across the paper—smooth, flat, and unadorned. So different from Somalia where color and texture pulsed through the land.

He remembered playing with his friends, pushing a metal wheel with a forked stick down the dirt street in front of his home. For a second, he felt the intense heat of the African sun on his skin.

"Will you draw pictures of Somalia on your poster?" his classmate asked. "My mom said people are fighting there. Were you scared?" Her eyes were as large as five senti coins.

Covering his head, Warfa tried to forget, but the images that fell upon him were like the heavy rains of the monsoon season. The sharp bang of a gun. The crumpled body of his neighbor. On the road, a man, his face covered. His long gun pointing at Warfa. Warfa trembled and waited for the memories to fade.

Safe at home, Warfa still waited.
"What's wrong my little lion?"
Grandma asked.

"I have to make a poster."

"Why are you worried?" Grandma cut up some goat meat, scraped it into a bowl of rice, and added cumin and coriander. "You're a good artist."

"It has to be about me. When I try, in my head, I see the man...with the gun...I can't breathe." Tears spilled down Warfa's cheeks. Grandma patted his back.

"One man fears fire; another man fears ashes. It is an old proverb. The gunman you saw in Somalia was fire. Everyone fears fire. But, your memories are ashes. They can't hurt you. If you touch ashes, they won't burn."

"It's art time," the teacher said. "Please take out your posters."
The other children eagerly snatched up their markers and began to draw.
Warfa stared at the markers for a long time before he chose one. He drew a thick
blood-red line down the center of his poster. Then another. And another.

Warfa's heart pounded like a djembe drum. His breath came out in jagged gasps. The cold hard rifle barrel was all he could see.

Dizzy and light-headed,
the marker slipped from his
fingers and clattered onto the floor.
"Is something wrong?" his teacher asked.
"Are you sick?"

On the way home, Warfa told Grandma what happened.

Grandma and Warfa sat down at the kitchen table. Grandma held his hands and said, "When you're afraid, take a deep breath in. Pretend you are smelling the flowers of the acacia tree." Grandma drew in a deep breath, closed her eyes, and smiled. She exhaled slowly. "Then, breathe out, like you are blowing a feather across the African savannah."

Warfa and Grandma practiced breathing.

The next morning, Warfa
begged to stay home.
"Remember the proverb."
Grandma said.

"I'll put a picture of fire
and ashes on my poster.
It will remind me that
memories are ashes.
They can't hurt me."

The whole time
Warfa worked
on his poster,
his belly hurt.

He imagined breathing in the scent of the acacia tree flowers. He envisioned blowing the feather clear across his classroom.

Deep breaths, in and out, slowly. Warfa added another image to his poster.

It was poster day. Warfa's bellyache returned.
"Who wants to go first?"
Warfa slumped in his seat.

His teacher beckoned him.

Warfa picked up his poster,
inched to the front of the room,
and stared at his shoes.

"Tell us about your poster." Warfa wanted to run. His breath was shallow and fast, and his stomach hurt more than ever. He stared at his poster. There, in the corner, was the tiny picture of fire and ashes.

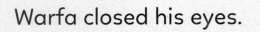

Warfa closed his eyes.

He breathed in the scent of the acacia flower, willing his racing heart to slow. Then, he thought about the feather and exhaled. "Not fire. Just ashes," Warfa whispered to himself.

He took a deep breath. As he blew out, his fear floated away. He unclenched his fists and forced the words out of his mouth.

"I...I am Warfa. I used to live in Somalia."

After school, Warfa rushed into his grandma's arms. "I did it. I shared my poster. I shared myself!"

"I knew you could, my little lion!"

Warfa smiled as big
as Africa.
"Roar!"

Authors' Notes

FIRE AND ASHES is the debut work in a series of children's books that focuses on mental health and self-care by featuring the wisdom found in African proverbs. Traditionally, these proverbs were handed down from generation to generation; however, many native Africans have moved away from their ancestral lands and settled elsewhere. Through these stories we hope to help immigrants and refugees regain a piece of their culture and be able to access and share the wisdom stored in these proverbs.

Proverbs make abstract and complex principles concrete and accessible, while also sharing knowledge learned from common human experiences. Proverbs impart awareness and understanding to children in a concise and often visual way.

In this African proverb series, we use the messages in these proverbs to help children make choices, take action, and overcome challenges.

Ahmed Hassan & Wes Erwin

The Power of Proverbs

There are 65.3 million refugees worldwide according to the Office of the United Nations High Commissioner for Refugees (UNHCR, 2016). Nearly a third of these refugees are children. At the end of 2020, approximately 2.65 million refugees from Somalia were displaced internally and another 522,000 in other countries (UNHCR,2020). Anxiety and post-traumatic stress disorder (PTSD) are common mental health issues for refugees.

Children in war-torn nations like Somalia experience trauma in large numbers. Often, their trauma is overlooked. This book focuses on only one type of impact that war has on children. Because of a child's more limited capacity to understand what is happening both internally and externally, and because of their lack of power to affect change, these children struggle to make sense of their circumstances.

The purpose of this book is to help children understand and differentiate between rational and irrational emotions and thoughts, and to help them adopt ways to cope through intentional breathing. We hope this practice will contribute to the process of healing and will help children better understand their trauma.

Warfa's grandmother uses an African proverb to illustrate ways Warfa can work through his trauma. She encourages Warfa to use the imagery of fire and ashes to understand the difference between an actual threat and his memories. The power of proverbs is strong in every culture. They are the knowledge and wisdom from countless generations distilled and expressed in a way that brings enlightenment and understanding.

Although this book is about a refugee child, the strategies presented are not limited to refugee populations. These are healthy coping strategies for any child who has experienced trauma.

We hope this story serves to educate, inspire, and entertain our readers.